D0520125

DESIGN
and decorate
LIVING ROOMS

Adams Media Corporation
Holbrook, Massachusetts

Lesley Taylor
with Jill Blake

Copyright © 1998 in text Lesley Taylor
Copyright © 1998 in photographs New Holland (Publishers) Ltd except those listed on
page 78
Copyright © 1998 in artwork New Holland (Publishers) Ltd
Copyright © 1998 New Holland (Publishers) Ltd

All rights reserved. No part of this publication may be reproduced, stored in a retrieval
system, or transmitted in any form or by any means, electronic, mechanical, photocopying,
recording or otherwise, without the prior written permission of the publishers and
copyright holders.

This edition published by Adams Media Corporation
260 Center Street
Holbrook, MA 02343
by arrangement with New Holland (Publishers) Ltd.
ISBN 1-55850-840-6

A B C D E F G H I J
CIP information available upon request from the publisher.

Printed and bound in Singapore

Contents

Introduction

Designing and decorating your living room should give many hours of pleasure, both in the creation and the enjoyment afterwards. This is the room where you are likely to spend a great deal of time sitting and relaxing so it is important that its ambience is conducive to this. But deciding on what style suits you best and how you should set about recreating it can be very difficult and this is where *Design and Decorate Living Rooms* comes into play.

Armed with this book you can first learn how to work out your needs and make the best use of your space in practical terms. Of course, it is difficult to plan exactly what you need if you are still undecided as to your preferences for the finished decor. The core of this book is given over to helping you, as the Style File on pages 10-59 takes a close look at a great number of different kinds of living room. Ranging from contemporary to country, and traditional to studio living, each section looks in depth at a selection of rooms. The text discusses the main decorative features and, more importantly, how you can achieve the same look in your own home.

The Focus File on pages 60-77 elaborates on the more practical elements of decorating a room. It concentrates on upholstery and soft furnishings, storage, walls and floor coverings, fireplaces and focal points, and lighting. Each aspect of the Focus File is written with the home decorator in mind, giving essential and realistic advice so that you can confidently create a truly stylish living room of your own.

Successful room layouts

The living room usually fulfills more than one purpose — it is used as a family room, for entertaining guests, for relaxing, reading and watching television, and for listening to music. Often it also has to double as a dining room — or even a study or guest room. Consequently, the layout and planning must be as flexible as possible.

Because living rooms are often designed as dual-purpose rooms, they are often long and thin, with a dining area at one end, and sitting area at the other. In older properties, this may have been achieved by removing a wall between two separate rooms (installing a roof-strengthening, rolled steel joist if the wall was load-bearing) to create an open-plan space. If you are considering doing this, think carefully before rushing to knock down a wall. Although you will get more natural daylight, and there will be a feeling of greater space, two separate rooms can be more cozy. They can also reduce family conflict — and it is easier to shut the door on one cluttered area than to be continually tidying up a large space.

With a long or fairly large room, it is practical to divide the space into sitting and dining areas, or conversation and television-watching areas. Do this with the clever positioning of furniture, rather than by creating permanent divisions. For example, a sofa can be placed at right angles to a main wall, facing the sitting area. Then position a second sofa or chair at right angles to the main sofa, or facing it (possibly across a coffee table?) to create a conversation corner. Two sofas, or a sofa and sofa bed, and/or several different, comfortable chairs are much more attractive to look at than the conventional three-piece suite. They are also easier to arrange and clever coordination can be achieved with the choice of upholstery.

A sideboard or other storage/serving surface could be positioned back-to-back with the sofa, facing towards the dining end of the room, for easy access to the dining table. Don't forget to allow space for opening doors/drawers on such items, or pushing back dining chairs from the table. There should still be enough space for a person to pass between chair and storage piece, while preferably still being able to open doors or drawers.

In such rooms, there are often one or even two chimneys

FORMAL SYMMETRY
▼ The symmetrical arrangement of the furniture and accessories in the entrance to this bay window creates a formal look — perfect for such a traditional setting.

DIVISIONS

▲ A screen can form a useful division in a large living area; alternatively, it can help break up a plain expanse of wall.

with recesses to each side, even if the fireplaces have been removed. Make full use of these recesses for storage purposes, with free-standing or built-in storage units at the lower level — these might house the television set or items for the dining table — and shelves above. The shelves could be flexible (supported on wall-mounted, adjustable brackets) or glass-fronted to display and store precious items. In some dual-purpose rooms, one recess can be used as a work area, with a desk or bureau at the lower level, and shelves above.

If you want to create a slightly more definite division between the two areas, consider using a portable folding screen, floor-to-ceiling curtains or vertical Venetian blinds.

Most living rooms need a focal point. Plan similar storage facilities and seating to those described above, even if there is only one chimney area. You could make a blank wall more interesting with fitted cabinets, leaving space in the center for a gas or electric fire, or an eye-catching display item. The seating can then be grouped around this.

If there is a beautiful view from a window, you might well prefer to use it as the room's focal point, especially in summer. Group seating around it, but don't block the access to the yard if the window is the main exit route.

As with all rooms, there is really only one way to plan the layout efficiently, and this means making a floor plan to scale, so you can see exactly how the furniture will fit. This looks like a bird's-eye view of the space. Measure it accurately, then draw out the room shape, on graph paper if possible (it is easier this way), making one square on the plan equal to one unit of floor space. For example, if you draw a 1:50 scale plan, this means that 1 inch on the plan equals 50 inches of the actual floor space. Show recesses, projections, doors and door swings (the way they open), radiators, windows, and anything else that is relevant.

COZY CORNER
▲ A small corner has been used to good advantage by filling it with a cozy seating arrangement. An extending wall lamp provides light to what could otherwise be a rather dark area; it is also ideal for reading.

Then use a separate sheet of graph paper to draw and cut out templates of your existing, or proposed, items of furniture. Remember to use the same scale and move the templates about on the plan until you are happy with the arrangement. You might like to color-code these, with one set of templates to represent existing items and a different color for proposed purchases.

If you want to be totally professional and make a clearer plan, trace off the plan/furniture in ink using tracing paper. Always write the scale, eg 1:20, 1:50, on the plan. You can then work out your lighting plan (see pages 74-75) on a tracing paper overlay and you can make sure that the lighting is put in the right place — say, a fixture positioned over the dining table.

Similar scale plans can be made for walls (elevations) to allow you to work out shelving, storage, etc., and to enable you to see whether furniture will fit under window sills. The wall is drawn as a straight line, with windows, fireplaces and radiators shown flat to scale; furniture templates need to be drawn in profile, as well, and not as though they were seen from above.

STYLE *file*

There is a huge choice of styles from which to choose when decorating any part of your home, but for the living room the choice is especially wide. Do you want to emulate a country or townhouse dwelling? Is your preference for something more contemporary or perhaps for a more traditional, period feel?

Do you favor subtle shades that team well or bright, primary colors from opposite sides of the color wheel? Is your taste for simple, streamlined furnishings or for more ornate window treatments with pelmets and tiebacks? Do you like light, airy surroundings or want to nestle down into something a little more cozy and atmospheric? By answering these questions you will start to form ideas for how you would like your living room to look.

Bear all these considerations in mind as you set out on the decorating path and look through each of the sections on the following pages. This part of the book puts different styles into context and shows you how to recreate the ideas in your own living room. By taking a close look at the basic elements of walls, floors, lighting and soft furnishings, and by mixing style, texture and form, an overall picture emerges. With careful planning, a firm idea of what style you want to create, together with attention to detail, you will discover the pleasure of designing and decorating the living room of your dreams.

LOFT LIVING
▲ Loft spaces are frequently very bright and airy with a large proportion of wall space given over to windows. In this room, maximum play is made of the light by painting the walls and ceiling white. The dark blue in the furnishings and carpet successfully keeps the living area grounded.

TOP LEFT
Combine different patterns from the same palette of colors. Here, classic furnishings are brought a touch of modernity through the boldly striped sofa.

BOTTOM LEFT
A collection of ethnic artifacts and pictures sets the theme. This living room's decor is simply created with suitable furnishing fabric and rugs.

TOP RIGHT
Pale, natural and light painted wood teams with cream-colored furnishings in this eclectic yet calming mix of styles. Red-brown accents provide a warm touch.

BOTTOM RIGHT
Successful color scheming here uses warm aqua blue as the dominant color, offset with a lesser quantity of pale yellow to add contrast.

Contemporary living

PLAINLY UP TO DATE
▲ A plain backdrop is the perfect foil for dramatic pieces of contemporary art and shapely furniture.

Contemporary style means "of today" and almost anything goes. The style can be frankly modern and minimalist, post-modern or even hi-tech, all of which have their origins in the Arts and Crafts movement at the end of the last century, the work of the architect Le Corbusier in the 1920s and the Bauhaus movement of the 1930s. The aims of all three were to combine the use of natural materials and well-made products with the technology of the machine age.

There are also many other current influences from Europe and from the U.S., where the loft space look, the Californian beach house and Shaker style are proving inspirational. Additionally, Oriental — especially Japanese — style is setting a new pared-down trend, and the ancient Chinese art of location and orientation, *feng shui*, is being considered more and more.

But the name 'contemporary' has also come to be associated with a simple, uncluttered Scandinavian look. This first became popular in the 1950s after the post-war rash of angular forms, riotous patterns and bold primary colors. Now the look has returned in a more restrained form, using pale colors and woods, natural textures and subtle paint finishes. Above all, the furniture is functional, often fulfilling more than one purpose, leaving the room uncluttered.

Contemporary style can also be highly individual, with the "shell" of the room decorated simply while making bold use of color in the furniture and furnishings. Shapes assume a greater importance, especially when used to make a dramatic statement.

ONE-COLOR LIVING

▶ By using a monochromatic color scheme teamed with simple ornaments and furnishings, a traditional setting is given a modern look.

TANTILIZING TEXTURES

▼ Wonderful textures and splendid plant specimens combine to create a living room of immense variety and interest.

Animal prints add flair
to a neutral scheme

STARK CONTRASTS
▲ Black and white patterns are supremely striking when set in a simple, monochromatic color scheme.

NATURALLY RESTRAINED
▼ Subtle patterns are introduced through the patina of natural wood, textiles and fruits.

This style can be used to create a room in which it is easy to relax after a hard day's work. The seating is arranged in a comfortable U-shape, to ease conversation, and grouped around a low-level coffee table, which is also used for storage. The coffee table, positioned in front of the seating, is an essential part of the style, and was adapted in the 1950s from a sofa table (which used to be positioned at the back, or drawn up to the side of the sofa for games, say, or to support lamps).

The soft, neutral colors give an impression of space and cool calm. The beiges, creams and off-whites with bleached woods rely on interesting textures and sharply defined contrast of form, to create a stylish sitting room. Even the radiator is colored to blend unobtrusively into the background. If you choose to paint your radiator to match the background wall, avoid oil-based paints as the colors will stain in time.

Pattern in this contemporary setting is restrained, being confined to an upholstered chair and two geometric abstract pictures, which are not particularly dominant as they are all part of the monochromatic scheme, and thus blend into the background. Instead, tonal contrast is achieved by the darker floor color, strikingly contrasting patterned cushions and stripped natural wood window frames — a model of understatement.

The window treatment, too, is simple, with neat, narrow-slatted miniblinds that can be angled to diffuse the daylight. Night lighting is provided by pools of light cast from the lamps on the glass storage chests to each side of the sofa, and by wall-washers, which bathe the paintings in a warm glow. Houseplants are used to provide a crisp green accent — very much an integral part of the Scandinavian look.

NEUTRALS

▼ Soft, neutral colors create a sense of calm and peace. Mix beige, buttermilk and oyster colors with bleached woods, using accessories such as plants to provide contrast.

New chic with crimson,
black and

**CREATIVELY
COLORFUL**

▼ The imaginative use of vibrantly colored glass in many different forms, brings a plain contemporary background vividly to life.

A bold, open-plan living area is typical of a metropolitan contemporary style, and works particularly well in apartments, converted warehouses and loft spaces. The textures are all modern in feel — shiny chrome, marbled flooring, glassware and glazed pottery, natural woven fabrics, leather and suedes – offset by plain, matte-painted walls and ceiling. Some contemporary interior designers like to make use of glossed surfaces, especially ceilings, to make a greater play of lighting. In this setting, however, there would have been far too much reflection from the

colored glass

flooring, and the chrome and glass shelves. You will find that combining matte and shiny surfaces is a valuable asset when varying texture in a living room.

The main decorations are neutral — creamy whites, greys and black — and the smooth flooring is laid in such a way as to help define the different areas in this large living space. This is further enhanced by the change in floor level. Even the main upholstery is monochrome, enlivened by bright red, contrasting cushions.

Vivid splashes of color add excitement to the scheme and provide a visual link that leads the eye from area to area. Standing by the seating space you are taken from the red cushions, to the larger-than-average picture and the collection of glass on the shallow glass shelves on the wall, to the unusual stained glass panels in the dining area.

The scheme relies on really good lighting for maximum impact. The glass shelves are lit from above by spotlights and from below with uplighters, and as light shines through the shelves, the collection is enhanced by interesting shadows cast on the wall behind. The picture is similarly highlighted by spot-lights set on the ceiling, while the stained glass panels are lit from behind. A floor-standing uplighter is a feature in its own right. This is the archetypal functional piece of furniture that makes a statement in its own right.

Unusual pieces of statuary and a feathery flower arrangement complete the scheme.

CONTRAST

▲ Black, white and red — three of the most strikingly contrasting colors — when combined with reflective and matte surfaces can achieve a visually stimulating interior.

Upbeat style with
tangerine

FOCUS ON FABRICS

▲ In a bold scheme such as tangerine and turquoise, use fabrics in sympathetic colors, but more muted shades.

BOLD COLOR

▶ Strong, bold colors work well in a contemporary setting where shapes are uncomplicated and lines are clean.

Many contemporary schemes rely on the clever use of color for maximum impact, especially when the budget is tight. This often means choosing complementary colors to create a visually stimulating look. Here turquoise and burnt orange — true complements of each other — have been used to stunning effect. The occasional table is painted pale turquoise to echo the color of the chair, making it an integral part of the scheme.

The setting is the top floor of a converted house, where an attractive arched window is the focal point. The seating is arranged to capitalize on this, and on the view over the rooftops. The window has been left uncovered as the room is not overlooked, while plants provide a subtle screen and will thrive in such light conditions. The room divider that separates the dining and sitting area is curved to echo the window shape, and helps to zone the two spaces.

The disparate pieces of furniture have tailored upholstery in a mixture of patterned and plain fabrics, all from the same color palette, that echo the turquoise, apricot and burnt orange theme. The patterns on the sofa and stool are restrained, which helps to define their individual shapes.

Being at the top of the building, the ceiling of the room is not very high. To make it seem higher, the walls are painted in a soft

and turquoise

golden yellow, a few tones paler than the floor, and the ceiling is an even lighter tone. This treatment of the main surfaces helps to create an impression of greater space and height, and unifies the strongly contrasting turquoise and orange.

Lighting is provided by standard and table lamps, which create low pools of light, while floor-mounted uplighters are used to cast light onto the ceiling at night, to help increase its apparent height. This treatment needs a well-plastered ceiling, otherwise any faults will be emphasized.

Accessories have been kept to a minimum and relate to the principal colors in the rest of the scheme.

BRIGHT LIGHT
▼ Such a fresh and zingy color scheme works especially well when there is plenty of natural daylight flooding into the living room.

Classical effect given
a contemporary

A first-floor living room in a typically tall turn-of-the-last-century town house has been given a simple, streamlined look, without losing its basic architectural character. The tall, elegant casement windows that open onto a balcony are dominant features, an impression that is emphasized by the picture and occasional table placed between them. The windows themselves have been treated very simply, with sheer drapes thrown over a pole to create swags and floor-length tails. A basic roller blind underneath can be pulled down for nighttime privacy, or on summer days to reduce the sun's glare.

The color scheme of this living room is a cool, neutral cream. With such large windows, the end result is a spacious airiness. To prevent the room from appearing too cool, the original pine floorboards have been retained. They were stripped and refinished and the warm, honey-colored end result is a perfect foil for the walls and soft furnishings. If your floorboards are not in especially good condition, consider liming or painting them instead. For a limed effect, brush on a wash of diluted white matte latex paint. For an aged effect, sand back the surface.

To add yet more warmth to this room, accent colors have been incorporated. The geometric wall hanging, cushions ranged along the sofa, and the charming floral painting are predominantly red with additional touches of yellow. Both of these colors come from the warm side of the color wheel and

HARD VS SOFT
▼ Cool crisp cotton ticking, hard slate tiles, soft flowing muslin and a smooth wooden picture frame provide a wide range of contrasting textures to add interest to the room.

treatment

so counterbalance the coolness of the rest of the decor.

A spacious room such as this with a few, well-chosen pieces of furniture benefits from some other accessories. These need not be small. To retain the minimalist, contemporary style, the owners of this particular room have chosen a simple potted tree to help bring the outdoors in and to create an additional spot of color. In the opposite corner of the room, there is also a rather splendid statue whose peaceful countenance can only bring calm and serenity to all who look at it.

WHITE LIGHT
▲ The windows are dressed with the bare minimum of draped muslin, allowing enough natural light to emphasize the contrasting hard, soft and shiny surfaces within the room.

Country style

Many people prefer a less formal style of living, especially if they live in a country cottage, converted barn or warehouse where natural materials have been used in the building, and are left unadorned. But this look can be created equally well in a bland, box-like living room to give it warmth and character, and a patina of age. This style relies on lots of natural and rustic tex-

FLORAL PARADISE

▲ A room filled with flowers — on fabrics, carpets, and in pots and vases — is the epitome of country and cottage style.

tures, such as exposed brickwork, ceiling beams, slate, quarry tiles, waxed floorboards, woven fabrics, cane and basketwork, and earthenware.

Pattern, provided in accessories, wall hangings, or small upholstered items, is usually kept to a minimum, but patterned curtains can help soften heavier textures. When pattern is used it should be traditional, such as florals, geometric motifs, basic checks, tartans or stripes. Colors are definitely natural and neutral, with extra earthtones added for warmth and impact.

Walls are often bare plaster, but can be painted with a matte-finish paint, or colorwashed for a softer look, and to suggest texture. Window treatments are usually simple, too, but when the window is attractive, leave it unadorned, or pull down a simple roller or Roman blind for privacy.

Accessories provide textural interest in the form of black wrought iron, antique brass, verdigris effects and large stoneware pots. Light is provided by table and standard lamps, wall lights, and possibly some very discreet concealed lighting, but nothing too intrusive, such as spotlights or downlighters.

INFORMAL SEATING

▶ Wooden paneling combined with Regency stripes and other period details are transformed into a suitably country style through the informality with which they are combined.

DIVIDED UP

▼ With the clever use of homey patchwork fabrics, lace and embroidery, as well as plants and old-fashioned pictures, this open-plan room is given a warm, country feel.

Soft furnishings medley
create rustic charm

DASHING DISPLAY

▲ If you are without a mantelpiece and want to create something similar, search out a simple shelving unit and display ceramics, glass, or any other objects that you cherish.

The rustic look perfectly complements this country cottage interior, being typical of the timber-framed buildings of hundreds of years ago. This method of building construction is becoming popular again and is well worth considering if you want to create a rustic-style living space.

The ceiling beams are exposed and sealed with a matte finish. (Never paint, stain or creosote old beams as this spoils their natural texture and color.) A mantel shelf is added above the fireplace to tone. The chimney area and walls are simply plastered and painted off-white — as is the plaster between the ceiling beams — with the brick interior of the fireplace left exposed.

Individual pieces of comfortable upholstered furniture are gathered around this inviting focal point, and are covered in different fabrics. The simple striped woven ottoman cover, the striped and coordinating floral chintzes on the small armchair and ample, buttoned sofa work well together. Conventional three-piece suites and all-matching items do not work if you want to create a rustic look.

The original tiled floor is covered in Oriental rugs — dyed in warm, earthy colors — to provide comfort underfoot. When used on hard floors, such rugs should always have a non-slip backing to prevent "creeping and curl" and to avoid accidents. If the rugs are colored using natural dyes, a backing will also prevent staining of the floor beneath.

CAREFULLY
CREATED
◀ A very inviting living room has been created through soft and comfortable funishings, a plethora of well-positioned pictures and other accessories, and subtle lighting.

The accessories are chosen to further enhance the rustic theme. The pictures on colored mounts, all similarly framed, draw attention to the fireplace. The circular occasional tables are covered with textured woven throws, in similar colors to the upholstered stool, and are used to display a cherished collection. When the lamps are lit, they cast pools of light onto these objects, highlighting the pictures mounted on the chimney area, and bathing the entire seating area in a warm and welcoming glow.

FABRIC
HALLMARKS
▼ Soft velvets, brocades and fringed braids in muted colors are hallmarks of the country look.

Simple elegance from
a country interior

In this all-neutral rustic setting, the look is one of a Tuscan farmhouse — a cool retreat from the hot summer sun. The wood of the ceiling beams and recess shelves has been bleached to creamy whiteness; the walls are painted plaster and the floors, doors and window frames have been left natural.

This monochromatic scheme helps to create an impression of space and elegance in a fairly confined area, and can be warmed up, or cooled down further, by the addition of specific color accents and accessories. Depending on your preferences, consider draping a brightly colored throw casually over one of the

SIMPLE CHOICES

▼ White on cream is not a color combination that immediately springs to mind, but actually white looks crisper when set against cream.

chairs; add piles of cushions — or perhaps just one, jewel-bright bolster — to the sofa; introduce a wall hanging, or display a collection of objects gleaned from your travels.

The upholstered furniture in this living room relies on an unusual shape — clearly defined by plain covers — to add visual impact, which is echoed in the large stoneware pots filled with rustic twigs. The covers for the furniture are loose fitting for ease of care and yet also tailored to give the neat finish that is the essence of this room.

The subtlest of pattern interest is added in the checked and striped throws, and some muted color in the terracotta planters. Apart from that, the living room is created around the interplay of different textures: worn wood abounds, the fabric is all self-patterned and the terracotta pots have the wonderful patina of age. Even the walls have retained their pitted, lumpy surfaces. Distemper paint, which is becoming increasingly easy to buy, is the perfect foil for walls such as these. Distemper creates a permeable surface and so does not trap dampness in aging walls.

This more sophisticated version of the rustic look could be created almost anywhere, in town or country, and would be particularly effective in a seaside or ocean setting. On a practical note, very pale schemes and upholstery are not especially suitable for family living. Good interior design must allow for a combination of the practical and the aesthetic.

BARE BRANCHES
◀ Branches collected in mid-winter and displayed in a simple white container with florist's foam are a striking addition to an interior such as this. The foam is concealed with scrunched-up tissue paper.

Personal style

Interior design and decoration can be a highly personal affair. Many people like to create an entirely individual look to stamp their own personality on their surroundings. They prefer to build an eclectic mix by collecting furniture, fabrics, cushions, ornaments, artifacts and other accessories over a period of time.

Adding a personal touch can be an inexpensive way of creating a stunning design scheme. It is also a good way of converting rented or company accommodation into a real home, even if there are restrictions on what can be done with the decorations and furniture. Fabrics, throws, rugs, pictures and accessories will all help you achieve the desired result — and they can be taken away with you when you move on.

The result can be one of inspired flair, perhaps brought about by using simple blocks of bold color against a neutral background. Or think about using various paint finishes and techniques to add that individual touch. A small room with objects and furniture painted with nautical motifs, for example, will suggest a narrow boat. Stenciled and painted patterns work well in most situations, and add design interest without the need to hang wallpaper. Floors can be similarly treated, or painted to suggest a rug (or use a heavy canvas for this, so that it does not become a permanent fixture).

The patterns and textures provided by fabrics are an easy — and even less permanent — way of creating a highly personalized interior, while pictures will always remain an important way of adding an individual touch.

JUNGLE LIFE
▼ Ethnic accessories sit very comfortably against a yellow background. The palm tree provides an authentic finishing touch.

TRUE DRAMA

▶ Paint effects are a great way of adding a truly personal touch to your living room. They can be as dramatic — as here — or as subtle as you like. If you don't like the end result, all you need to do is paint over it.

DRAMATIC STATEMENT

▼ This living room is certainly making a dramatic statement. Noel Coward and a pillar-box red piano dominate the background, while the glass-laden coffee table and svelte leopard-skin cushions bring drama to the seating area.

Colorful impact with
striking

ALL MIXED UP
▼ Take primary colors, mix them together, add a touch of black and you end up with a striking living room.

A classic interior with Art Deco overtones is decorated mainly in neutral colors — off-whites, beiges and creams — that enhance the natural wood parquet floor. Impact is added by colorful furniture and accessories, at the same time creating contrast in style and form that is echoed in the curving handrail and the shapely pillars. Such schemes need textural contrast to give them more of a lift, which is here provided by the rug, mirror, wrought iron and wood.

Attention is drawn to the focal point — the fireplace — by the use of bold blocks of color on the well-positioned wine-red

soft furnishings

upholstered chaise and the blue and coral duvet-style sofas. Strong yellow accents, incorporated by the table top and by the ceramic dish on the coffee table, add a sunshine touch. The frieze, just below ceiling height, is painted to reflect these colors. This all helps to give a more cozy, inviting feel to this large and rather clinical space.

JEWEL BRIGHT
▲ A few cushions covered with plain, bright fabrics, may be all that you need to create a similar effect.

Bookshelves and units built into the main wall provide adequate streamlined storage. At the same time, they also add a colorful touch to a blank wall. Pictures and accessories further enhance the look.

Subtle accent lighting is provided to emphasize specific areas. Wallwashers bathe the fireplace, bookshelves and pictures in a soft glow, while downlighters create a star-studded impression in the lowered ceiling. Setting halogen lights into a ceiling need not necessarily mean hours of labor. They can be installed by simply cutting appropriate-sized holes in the ceiling. Ask an electrician to do this for you.

This look would not be too difficult to create in a smaller space, using single chairs or even bold floor cushions to supply the blocks of color. Pictures, books and other accessories that are already an integral part of the room's contents can be rearranged to create an impact. It can be very time-consuming deciding what pictures hang where and the best way to combine them. But perservere, and you will find the best solution.

Edwardian splendor
in sumptuous scarlet

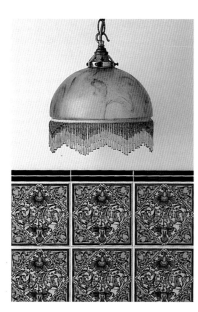

ACCESSORIZE
▲ Period wallcoverings and accessories can readily be found as reproduction pieces if you don't want the trouble or expense of locating originals.

ADDED VALUE
▶ For a sense of history, seek out old photographs, shields, emblems and other memorabilia to display on the walls of your room.

The cluttered look of a Victorian or Edwardian turn-of-the-century parlor is recreated by a scheme colored in warm, inviting tones. It is further enhanced by plenty of contrasting cushions on plump, well-stuffed upholstery, and an unrestrained mixture of patterns and accessories.

In summer, the room is arranged rather like a caravan, barge, or even Queen Victoria's personal royal train, with the seating curved in front of the tiled fireplace. In winter, it would be better to rearrange the furniture so that the fireplace becomes a warm and welcoming focal point for the seating.

The heavily patterned upholstery fabric (offset by rich, red-painted walls) is also used for the tailored Roman blinds at a small side window, and for the full-length drapes with fabric valance, suspended from a brass pole at the main window. In addition, both windows have sun-screening blinds which can be pulled down (as did the Victorians) to prevent sunlight from encroaching and fading the carpets and furnishings.

Blinds like this are especially valuable in a south-facing room as fabrics are destroyed all too quickly by the sun.

The carpet has a traditional pattern, which could be reproduced on a floorcloth or even as a design stenciled

GOOD HUNTING
◀ An eye for detail and
the ability to fill a room
such as this with myriad
suitable objects fleshes
out a nostalgic feel.

directly onto the floorboards. The colors are mercifully muted; too much red and the room would be overpowering. The small, brighter colored patches, make it a part of the whole, however.

The accessories and light fittings have been particularly well chosen to follow the Victorian theme. The framed tennis racket and collection of cups, the potted aspidistras and parlor palms, the touches of Benares brassware and the canopied standard lamp all complete the scene.

This might be too heavy a treatment for a smaller setting, where the color and patterns could be claustrophobic, but a similar look can be achieved with paler tones and a more subtle blend of patterns.

Tex-Mex living uses
a simple approach

Specific fabrics, patterns, textures and colours can be combined to create an African or Arabian ambience. Transform a conventional living room to suggest sparse, wide open plains, nights on safari under star-studded skies, or sleeping in canvas tents with cozy woven blankets.

HOT NIGHTS
▶ The roughly textured walls suggest desert climes.

to decor

Here, the ceiling has been removed and the beams and joists exposed. They have been stained a warm, sunburnt brown and sealed with a matte varnish. The walls have been roughly plastered — reminiscent of mud walls and desert sand — and the plaster has also been used to form a curving hole-in-the-wall fireplace.

The chosen colors enhance the theme — subtle earth and sand tones for the pale yellow walls and deeper ocher upholstery, together with sun-bleached terracotta and dusty palm green. The fabrics for the cushions and throws are authentic woven kilims, but they could be copied in an ethnic-type print. The end result could be a lot softer and less scratchy, too.

The tall sash windows are fitted with wooden Venetian blinds that can be angled to control the light, and conceal the urban view (as well as the curious gaze of passersby). To soften them, unbleached muslin swags are held in place by swag holders, fixed to the tops of the windowframes.

Potted cacti and other greenery in terracotta pots, pieces of pottery, sun-bleached wood and sheepskin rugs all provide a textural mix, as does the wall-mounted ram's head. Spotlights on a track are angled to emphasize these features at the flick of a switch. These lights might be the perfect candidate for dimmer switches. Bear them in mind when planning your scheme.

PLANT DETAILS
◀ Never underestimate the use of plants in an indoor scheme. Here, the cactus is the perfect partner to Tex-Mex living.

ETHNIC PRINTS
▼ Woven kilims or mock ethnic print throws are a quick way to create the look here. Usually made of pure cotton or wool, they wear well and are often inexpensive.

Traditional living

**PERFECTLY
PERIOD**
▼ Regency stripes, a
well-dressed wicker sofa
and beautiful floral
prints transform this
living room into a truly
traditional setting.

The English classic country house look is currently the height of decorating chic for living rooms, and is envied and copied all over the world. It is a look that works well in a genuine country setting, where it might be scaled down to become "country cottage" style, but is equally at home in an urban setting, where it will bring a breath of fresh air.

The country style relies on contrast of texture and form; muted color schemes; interesting and varied accessories that are well grouped; beautifully draped window treatments, and lots of plants and stunning flower arrangements. The room is then further enhanced with pools of light from table and standard lamps, combined with subtle window lighting.

The end result should look as though the room has been built up over many decades. Furniture can be an eclectic mix, some of it genuine antiques, together with possibly a few reproduction pieces, and other items painted and/or distressed to look as though they are old and part of the whole. Tables may be skirted with fabric and older pieces of upholstery concealed under a throw, and masses of differently shaped cushions piled on sofas and chairs. Covers may well be loose and easy-to-clean: linen-cotton union, in a floral pattern, is a classic favorite.

Walls are often painted and can have a "split-level" treatment of dado, chair rail, infill, picture rail, frieze and cornice or coving. This works well in large, tall rooms, helping to reduce the apparent height. If the walls are papered, the pattern should be a classic Regency stripe, heraldic design or full-blown floral.

TRUE BLUES
▶ Blue and white is a traditional favorite color combination. Here, collections of blue and white china coordinate with eclectic upholstery.

FORMALITIES
▲ A traditional room graced by a beautiful bowed window is given a classic treatment with antique furniture, full-length window drapes and a rich floor covering.

Classic symmetry and
a restful color scheme

Green is one of the most effective colors to use to bring a breath of country air into the living room, and it will also help to make a small space look larger. To magnify the effect, use light-reflecting surfaces, such as gloss paint; glazed chintz; silky or foil wall coverings; a mirror; touches of brass. Add contrast and emphasis with some rustic touches, such as cane and basket-ware, terracotta pots, woven fabrics or homespun rugs.

This crisp, mainly neutral, monochromatic scheme is enlivened by green accents and accessories. Never underesti-mate the use of green houseplants to add a country ambience to

**PEACE,
PERFECT
PEACE**

▶ Green, in these subtle shades, is a most soothing and relaxing color. By choosing a timeless checked fabric that tones with the rest of the decor, you can create a restful living space. It is a room where you would want to spend plenty of time unwinding from the stresses of the day.

for relaxed elegance

a scheme, and to echo the garden beyond. This will create a cool look for summer; with a few subtle changes and the addition of some warm accents, the room can be transformed into a more cozy area for winter.

The pale wood picture frames highlighted with gold details and the collection of small baskets reflected in the mirror inject more warmth to the color scheme. The pale green mounts are a similar hue to the rest of the green used in the room's decor, further unifying the scheme.

Pattern is kept to a minimum, with smart checked fabric used for the neatly tailored covers for the two armchairs, which helps to define their simple form, and adds to the uncluttered look. The relatively small space is magnified visually by the large mirror over the fireplace. The mirror has been carefully chosen to reflect the elegant moldings in the coving running around the ceiling. Because the frame has been painted to match the rest of the woodwork, it is not too heavy an addition above the fireplace. A brown frame would have been considerably more imposing. The room's proportions are such that it benefits from a mirror of this height, but when choosing a mirror for your own room ensure that you don't buy anything that is too large.

The coordinating lamps and shades, the classic fireplace fender, and the formal arrangement of pictures and ornaments help to emphasize the fireplace as the focal point.

TINY TOPIARY
◀ Small topiary trees in terracotta pots are readily available in different shapes and sizes, and make an ideal decoration for a formal setting.

GREEN AND YELLOW
▼ Touches of bright yellow, in a room that is essentially decorated in green, gives the interior a lift.

Patterned and plain surfaces
a successful mix

DECOUPAGE

▲ Personalize your living room with old boxes that are treated with an antiquing paint effect and then covered with decoupage.

CLASSIC COMBINATIONS

▶ This decor relies on a rich combination of color and pattern. Mix terracotta, forest green or royal blue stripe wall-coverings with William Morris-style printed fabrics, and add architectural moldings if your room lacks these vital period elements.

All successful interior decorating schemes rely on a good balance between patterned and plain surfaces. Furthermore, the designs selected for these surfaces help to set the style, whether it be period or modern in context.

It is always important to choose a pattern that suits the size and shape of the surface on which it is to be used. Employ bold designs on large areas and discreet patterns on smaller surfaces. Also, plan the position of the pattern carefully so that you don't get any awkward cut-off points (tops of trees or flowers, or animal heads missing at the tops of walls or curtains). Also ensure that the main motifs are correctly centered, say above the backs of sofas and fireplaces. Take care with the strength of color too. Pale and medium-tones work best on smaller surfaces, whereas bolder ones can be used on large walls and floors, or at important windows.

In this warm, inviting living room, pattern has been used cleverly to create an impression of greater height. Vertical stripes help to "raise" the ceiling. The ceiling is painted the same color as the paler, soft rose background of the stripe — another visual trick to increase the height. Contrary to popular belief, white ceilings do not necessarily look higher, unless they are combined with white walls, or where the background to a wall covering is white.

The pattern mix has been cleverly coordinated. The striped drapes are slightly different

than the wallpaper, but from the same color palette, so they blend well with the walls and yet define the window recess. The checked and striped upholstery on the armchair and *chaise longue* act as a neutral link between wall and window treatments, the sofa and the formal geometric motifs on the floor.

The lighting is mainly provided by decorative lamps, in keeping with the style of the room. In addition, there is lighting on the ceiling and on the tables to enhance certain accessories.

VARIETY
◀ Texture has been considered carefully in this living room, with gilt frames, touches of alabaster and brass, and polished woods all contrasting with the matt walls, silky-striped *chaise* and a nubbly needlepoint rug.

Golden glow from
warm yellow and

Color is used to give a room mood, ambience and atmosphere, but it will also help to create a specific style, whether you are looking for a period setting or a modern one. Most country and town house settings tend to be more traditional in flavor, with good architectural features, and attractive furniture, that can be emphasized and enhanced by the clever use of color.

To create a traditional look, the colors chosen can be rich and inviting, adding warmth and sunshine to a cold, dark space, or more muted and faded with a combination of subtle warm and

NATURAL
▶WARMTH
 The warm tones of natural wood are in complete harmony with the saffron yellow walls. With occasional hints of blue, the end result is a warm and alluring living room.

mellow wood

mid-tone cool colors. Warm-toned, contrasting schemes work well in a fairly large space, or if a cozy, intimate atmosphere is required; monochromatic (one color or tone-on-tone) effects will help to enlarge a smaller room, and create an impression of elegance and space.

Here, the sunshine yellow walls blend well with the stripped pine doors and natural wood furniture, and the touches of brass and the gilt-framed mirror all help to give the room a welcoming golden glow. Often these sundry facets are forgotten when a color scheme is being planned, but it is essential to consider every surface to be decorated, and this includes the furniture and accessories as well as the walls, ceiling, woodwork, floor and window treatments.

A little green and blue for contrast, introduced in the curtain fabric, the checked table cover, pictures, cushions and glassware help to stress the overall warmth of the color scheme. Such complementary accents will bring a room to life, and define the main theme.

This would be an ideal scheme for a cold living room in a tall town house, or to add warmth to a dark drawing room in a country house — possibly made dark by the addition of an extension or conservatory.

The upholstery, cushions and covers have been cleverly chosen to unify the individual items of furniture. At the same time, they also provide pattern interest and textural contrast, and the rug further enhances the theme.

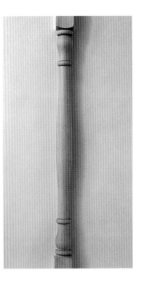

GOLDEN GLOW
▲ Yellow is a color guaranteed to gladden the heart. Teamed with natural wood, it will provide a warm glow even in the darkest of living rooms.

Period living uses
traditional furniture

SCREENED OFF
▲ The essential
Victorian-style
accessory is a screen
that keeps drafts at bay
and also helps
successfully to divide a
large living space into
smaller areas.

If your room already has a period architectural style, you will have the best possible starting point for creating a traditional living room. However, if you don't know where to begin, discover the age of the property (try the original deeds or house documents, or research in your local library); then look at books, and visit museums and historic houses or stately homes of the same period to give you some stimulating ideas. You will then have a far better idea of what is suitable — and, more importantly, what is quite unsuitable — for your living room. Now you can start to plan with greater confidence.

Here, a typically tall turn-of-the-century sitting room already has an attractive cornice and frieze with a picture rail below. These have been enhanced by painting the frieze in a soft lilac, to contrast with the pale green walls, and the cornice, ceiling and picture rail are picked out in white to add an extra strong emphasis.

The furniture is mostly typical of the period, and the tall bureau bookcase creates an imposing focal point; such large items were popular — and practical — during the closing decades of the last century, and they work well in lofty rooms. Contrast in height is as important as contrast of form when selecting furniture. It is necessary to provide extra visual interest on the vertical plane.

Contrast of form is provided here by the gently curving shape of the sofa, defined by the plain upholstery on the arms and base that contrasts with the patterned back and seat cushions.

and features

This is offset by the varied shapes of the occasional tables, set against the squares and rectangles of the other pieces.

Such rooms would have been impossibly cluttered in the Victorian era. Although this setting has been pared down for today's living, it may still be too fussy for some tastes (especially as most people do not have a team of servants to dust and clean), but this cozy, lived-in look is an integral feature of the style, and in many cases it could be provided by cleverly chosen, easy-to-clean accessories.

VIRTUALLY VICTORIAN
◀ A living room that retains period details is asking to be decorated in its original style. Large pieces of furniture, plenty of ornaments and rich colors are hallmarks of late 19th-century style.

Linear white and black
for a Gothic look

**CRISPLY
STYLISH**

▲ Wrought iron acces-
sories create strong
lines against the more
muted, linear patterns
of the soft furnishings.
For a less contrasting
look, you could try light
fittings in steely-grey
gun metal or an antique
brass finish.

Window treatments are usually a very important feature in a traditional living room, as the sitting or drawing room is frequently a more formal area in this type of property. As such, they should be designed to be in sympathy with the overall decorating theme and also to fit the proportion of the room.

The drapes in formal rooms should be full-length, unless the window is a really small, casement type, when sill-length curtains might be more suitable. If there is a radiator under the window, floor-length curtains can still be used and combined with blinds, which close for insulation and privacy, while the main drapes can be pulled back to the radiator's edge. This is one place where pelmets, valances, trimmings, tiebacks and decorative curtain rods come into their own, and will be an integral part of the window dressing, contributing towards their style.

In this room, with its Gothic flavor, the beautiful arched window is sympathetically treated to show off its shape to maximum advantage. The two curtains are suspended from cast iron rings on Gothic-style black iron rods, which are staggered in height above the top of the window, so that their curved tops can be fully appreciated when the drapes are pulled back during the daytime.

This theme is also followed through in other accessories — the wall lights and central chandelier, suspended above the seating area to add drama to the scene at night, and in the candle holders on the side table and desk. Other lighting is provided by simple table and standard lamps. All the light fittings and their accessories are in black and white to further enhance the Gothic look, and demonstrate how easy it is to set a specific style with cleverly chosen pieces. The brown ticking stripe is smart and the fabric hard-wearing. The padded coffee table has been covered in a similar striped fabric, but in black, to give a soft finish to balance the hard lines of the wrought iron.

To prevent the ceiling from becoming too overbearing, the beams and the joists between have been painted white instead of the more usual dark brown staining. The well-worn nature of the wood shines through so the room retains its character.

SIMPLY SMART
◄ A very smart country interior has been created by limiting the choice of materials — a mixture of hard wrought iron and soft furnishing fabrics.

Studio living

VERSATILITY
▲ A functional day bed and table mean that this studio appartment can quickly be transformed into a bedroom, dining room or office as the needs arise.

These days, studio living is trendy. Maximum use can be made of one large, well-lit, open space for living, sleeping, eating, dining, relaxing, and entertaining. This has partly been brought about by the shortage of living space and escalating property prices. Nowadays, many warehouses, factories, hospitals and other industrial spaces have been converted into studio living spaces. The top floors of these buildings may lend themselves to loft conversion since these areas usually have interesting architectural features like sloping ceilings, unusual windows and fine views.

The interior is often minimal, leaving the owner to add fixtures, furniture, storage and style according to personal taste. This means careful planning from the outset if you want to create a really workable space. Try to plan from the inside out. Work out what you need to accommodate and store, and decide how you can best divide the space so it will function practically. Divide the space into zones, so that one part of the space is used for dining, another for sitting and relaxing, and another for working. Try organizing the sleeping area so it has some privacy.

When it comes to choosing the decor, this type of space lends itself to bold treatments, since there are usually large areas that can take stronger colors and definite patterns. Remember to relate the size of the pattern and strength of the color to the scale of the surface on which it is to be used.

MAKING THE MOST OF IT

▲ This long, narrow room is cleverly zoned through the use of a blind that can be lowered beside the bed, and a table that can be drawn into the middle of the room.

SMALL SPACE LIVING

◀ In a more feminine approach, the bed in this studio flat has been raised and shelves incorporated to make a room within a room.

White and black
make strong statement

To live successfully in a small space, you need to make the most of every nook and cranny. Of course, if you are lucky enough to have a tall room, then there is the opportunity to move upwards as well as across the floor space, which is precisely what has been achieved here.

Making a room within a room is most frequently attained by the careful positioning of the furniture or by creating a division — either hard or soft. In this studio room, however, a bedroom has been made by building a raised area at one end of the room.

COOL AND CLEAR

▶ Minimalist living can only really be achieved if you have the storage space to accompany it. Here, large cabinets are incorporated into the raised platform sleeping area.

Cabinets are incorporated into the structure, thereby cleverly solving the other problem attached to small-space living — where to store everything.

To maximize space, as much clutter as possible should be ejected from the home, or at least stored away. Although creating storage areas might initially seem like a waste of valuable space, ultimately it is well worth it as it makes everyday living a great deal less cluttered and more straightforward.

The best way to create the illusion of space is to decorate the room in simple, pale colors. Don't draw in the walls or ceiling with dark reds, blues or greens, as this will only serve to make the place seem more claustrophobic. The fresh white paint on all the surfaces in this room make it look crisp and clean. The walls recede because they are not broken up with dominating pictures, or interrupted by shelves of knickknacks.

The few pieces of furniture are black, chosen to contrast stylishly with the white background. The gun-metal grey carpet is equally plain and smart, and it unifies the decor of the room very successfully.

Too much black and white might become difficult to live with, so the sleeping area at the top of the metal step ladder is softened with tungsten lighting, which gives off a warm yellow glow. This softening effect is further enhanced by the pastel shades of the bedding.

STRONG STATEMENT

▲ Never forget the strong statement that can be made by using all white with a touch of black or grey. Or follow a monochromatic theme with just these three colors. Accents can be provided by natural wood, terracotta or green plants.

Cream colored living
for night and day

Storage assumes enormous importance in a one-room-living situation. Everything must earn its place if the space is to function efficiently and living is not to be uncomfortable. This is where practical planning comes into its own.

Here an entire storage wall for books, television, video tapes, cassettes and CDs is used to create a room divider between the sitting and sleeping space and the dining/kitchen area. Companion shelves on the reverse side are used to store glasses, china and everything needed for cooking and the table. Mirrors magnify the space and give increased light.

MIRROR IT
▼ Shiny, reflective surfaces create a sense of spaciousness. Use mirrors wherever possible and lay a glossy floor covering, such as vinyl or polished wood veneer.

When storage like this is being planned, it is wise to measure the things you need to store (including assessing their weight) so you can ensure all shelves, cupboards and drawers are deep, tall, wide and strong enough to accommodate everything. This may mean having some adjustable shelves.

If you are faced with a situation of extreme clutter, it may be wise to call in an expert in built-in furniture, or a carpenter who can work to your specifications and tailor-make storage to your requirements. Alternatively, you could adapt ready-made storage yourself, perhaps incorporating adjustable shelves on wall-mounted slots, or metal scaffold-type or industrial shelving if you plan a hi-tech look.

The storage can be painted — as is done here — so it is unobtrusive and fades into the background. Alternatively, you could

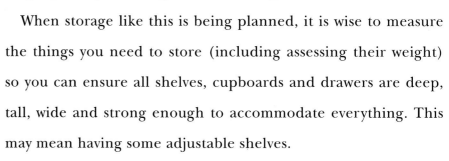
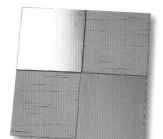
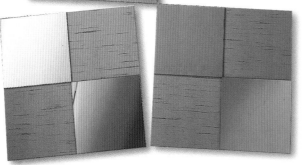

**VARIATION ON
A THEME**
◀ Although basically just
a studio apartment, this
living area has been
given a touch of class by
using traditional
furniture and furnishings
set in a sophisticated
cream color scheme.

paint it to contrast and stand out. This would work well in a hi-tech space, or if you wanted to unify disparate pieces.

The mainly neutral color scheme in this studio lightens the room, creates a tranquil atmosphere that helps to increase the apparent space, and leads to an uncluttered look. There is a good textural mix — the blond wood floor is softened by a large rug (which helps to divide the area into zones), and the bed has a practical fringed cover. The large potted plant adds extra visual detail and casts interesting shadows onto the wall and ceiling under artificial light.

Conservatory &

The garden room or conservatory often bridges the gap between the patio, terrace or verandah, and the main living room. It can be a separate extension to the house, used for summer living and dining, possibly filled with exotic plants and shrubs, or it may be an integral part of an existing room. It can be used to create a sense of space and all-year-round summer in a dark, overshadowed living room or gloomy basement.

BLINDED BY THE SUN

▲ Any conservatory or garden room that consists mainly of glass will need adequate shade. For a large room, electrically controlled blinds will be a worthwhile investment.

The decorations, furniture and furnishings may echo the theme of the main living area, or you can create a specific style more in keeping with the traditional conservatory. You may favor a "return to the Raj" look, for example, or a Shaker style with painted and distressed furniture, simple accessories and patchwork fabrics.

If you plan to extend a room in this way, ensure the glazing is adequate to provide good insulation, both from winter cold and summer heat — no one wants to shiver or fry when temperatures drop or soar. The ventilation will need to be carefully controlled, especially if the room is to contain exotic flora, and the heating should be equally efficient.

Some form of sun screening will also be essential. There are many companies that specialize in conservatory blinds and awnings. Canvas screening, which unfurls like a yacht sail, can be both practical and decorative.

In a garden room, lighting will have to be incorporated in the structure as discreet fixtures. Pools of light, thrown from table lamps and candles, are intimate and effective.

garden rooms

BRIGHT AND BREEZY

▶ Because of its many French windows and simple styling, this living room has the feel of a conservatory. Any room at the back of the house can be remod-elled by adding large picture windows or patio doors to create a garden living room.

FORMALITY PRESERVED

▼ Don't be limited to rattan or traditional "conservatory" furniture. This room is proof that it can look every bit as formal as a more conventional living room.

Say it with flowers

Here is a garden room extension with pretty floral fabric curtains, cushions and table cover, offset by plain blue sofas the color of a summer sky. This is a good way of mixing fabrics for a truly coordinated look.

The dominant fabric is the large floral design which has been used comparatively simply. The curtains are simply pleated and suspended from chunky white-painted wooden curtain rods, while the tablecloth has been left to hang straight to the floor, with only small pleats at each corner to neaten it. A piece of glass has been cut to fit the top of the table so that the fabric beneath is protected from accidental spillage. It is worth considering doing this in a living room where a tablecloth is on permanent display as liquids can easily spoil the surface. It is even more important if the fabric coordinates with other furnishings as washing more frequently will soon discolor the fabric.

When using such a heavily patterned fabric it is as well to keep its uses simple. The exceptions in this garden room are the two ruffled cushion covers on the sofas. The ruffles are delightfully frivolous and complement the plain sofa covers. The piping around the cushions, in the same fabric, successfully links the cushions to the seating.

The skylight in the pine-clad ceiling helps to emphasize the sunny

LUSCIOUS FLORALS

▼ Natural materials, such as stone and wood, are excellent backdrops to highly patterned floral fabrics.

aspect of the seating in the garden end of the room and enhances the country-style textures. Lighting by lamps and candles makes the most of the sitting area at night.

A capacious Edwardian sideboard is used for storage, and has been given a new lease of life with a distressed paint finish; the door panels have been stenciled with an appropriate floral motif. Such pieces are often available at a reasonable price from secondhand shops, auctions or car boot sales.

Flowers, plants and pictures all contribute to the country cottage style of decoration, which would work equally well in a suburban house, a formal town house, or a metropolitan apartment, creating an indoor/outdoor garden theme.

COUNTRY-STYLE COMFORT
▲ Country-style fabrics create a comfortable garden room in which to sit and look out at the view. Although the predominant color — pale blue — is from the cool side of the spectrum, it is warmed up by the wood-clad ceiling and touches of red in the curtains and tablecloth.

Letting in the light

This conservatory extension to a main living area leads out onto a terrace. Pale and sunshine colors ensure that maximum light is reflected into the darker original living space. The unusual fan shape of the extension is echoed in the curved form of the sofa and the cane chair, which also provides textural contrast and is enhanced by the feathery feel of the plants.

Night lighting is carefully considered with strategically placed spotlights incorporated into the outside wall of the living room. Uplighters are concealed among the larger plants to give a really effective, shadow-torn light as dusk falls. By day, too much

OUTDOOR LIVING
▼ With an extension like this, the living room is taken directly out into the garden.

light can be dazzling in a conservatory and if you are growing plants in there, the resulting heat will be overwhelming. In this room, sun screening is provided by neatly rolled blinds, which are electronically controlled from inside to unfurl individually to cover the glazed roof. As the ceilings of most conservatories are too high to reach comfortably, it is worth investigating the possibility of electronic blinds. There are, however, many other sorts of blinds. Consult an expert to give you the pros and cons.

Imaginative use has been made of the original house wall, which is partially retained and used to support a built-in bookcase. Any such structural building work must be done by a professional builder or conservatory contractor, as load-bearing walls will have to be strengthened to support the floors above. This may well involve the insertion of a roof strengthening joist. A structural engineer or surveyor will calculate to ensure the joist is strong enough to bear the load.

The addition of a conservatory or garden room extension may require planning permission. This is one good reason for employing a specialist contractor, as they are usually well versed in local planning rules, and will undertake to apply for permission on your behalf. A visit to your local authority Environmental Planning Department is worthwhile, to check for yourself.

CONSERVATORY GARDENS

▼ Tubs of green plants bring the outdoors inside. Select natural stoneware or terracotta pots for a more rustic look, or as a stark contrast in a modern setting.

FOCUS *f i l e*

Once you've had the opportunity to look at general styles of decoration, you will need to focus on the elements that make up the room of your choice. Over the following pages, we look at those parts of the living room that create the whole. The living room is not only a place to relax and sit in comfort, but it is also the one room that is seen most often by guests — a space in the home where you can show off your design and decorating skills in full force! The upholstery and soft furnishings you choose are vital to the overall look of the room; they must be both easy to maintain, yet attractive and in keeping with the style of decor. As these can be a costly purchase, you might find pages 62-67 well worth reading before selecting these most important elements of the room. Walls and floors are the largest areas of the room to be decorated, so decisions on paint, wallpaper, and floorcoverings are, again, of great importance. Recognising the style of decor is the first step, but then, what is the most effective option? The information on pages 68-71 should help you to decide.

Virtually every living room has a focal point. In colder climes, this is nearly always a fireplace; however, in warmer countries, it could be either a large picture window overlooking a beautiful view of an ocean bay, or a painting, mural or display cabinet. Wherever you live, or whatever style of decor you want to replicate, the section on Focal Points, on pages 74-75, makes interesting reading and offers tips on creating a focus to the room.

The living room also needs to house an assortment of per-

sonal and household items. Sideboards, display cabinets, wall units or freestanding cabinets are all discussed in detail on pages 74-75. They can be turned into a feature in their own right or integrated into the decor in an unobtrusive way.

Finally, adequate and attractive lighting is most necessary in the living room, where relaxation and entertainment feature strongly. Pages 76-77 explain how to plan for effective lighting,and explain why you need different lights in this multi-functional room.

LINES AND SQUARES
▲ Simple shapes and strong, basic colors are an effective but easy way to create a modern look.

Working with fabrics

It is the fabrics and soft furnishings that make a house into a home. In the living room, the upholstery, cushions, covers, window treatments and small accessories will help to create a cozy ambience, and give the owner a chance to imprint their personality on the scheme.

Above all, the upholstered furniture should be comfortable for everybody who is going to sit and relax in the living room. Some people like to sprawl in a softly upholstered sofa or chair, while others prefer a more upright position, with seating that is firmer to sit on, with good support for the head.

Take the room measurements with you when you shop (as well as color samples of any existing items like the carpeting), since there is no point in deciding on a large four-seater sofa only to find it won't fit into the space. Don't worry about choosing different pieces — you can always unify them by using the same fabric to cover all the items (most manufacturers and suppliers run a cover-in-customers'-own-fabric service), or use a coordinated range of fabrics to mix-and-match curtains, covers and cushions.

This is when a combination of plain and patterned fabrics come into their own. Use stripes or checks as a neutral link, and add contrast piping and trimmings in the same color palette to unify and define the shape of the furniture. In fact, a contrast of both texture

COMBINING SHAPES

▼ Cushion pads are made in all manner of shapes and sizes. Here, round and rectangular are combined to emphasize the geometric shape of this sofa.

and form is essential to successful interior design, and choosing disparate pieces can help to achieve this.

When deciding on upholstery, practical aspects have to be considered — what sort of wear and tear will the furniture receive? If the living room is used by young children and rambunctious teenagers, loose covers in a sensible color and hardwearing, easy-to-clean fabrics are usually a wise option. If the room is used mainly by adults, however, then paler colors, tight covers and more fragile fabrics could be chosen. But bear in mind that most seating does take a fair amount of punishment, so very pale colors and delicate textures are best avoided. It is wise to consider some form of stain protection for the main items of soft furnishings in your living room. Also, always check on the quality of fillings, and the flame retardancy of the upholstery and fabrics, to ensure they conform to safety standards and fire regulations.

When deciding on fabrics, aim to achieve a good balance between pattern and plain, and always remember to relate the size of any design and the strength of color to the scale of the surface on which it is to appear. Use large, flowing florals on well-rounded chairs and sofas; checks, stripes and geometrics on square or rectangular streamlined pieces; neat mini-prints and checks on small stools or dining chairs. The same rule applies to fabric for curtains and blinds. Plain fabrics are a wise choice for buttoned upholstery and curtains that have very decorative headings.

COLORFUL ADDITIONS
▲ Cushion covers are the perfect way to inject instant color and variation of pattern into a living room. If you are using lots of different patterns, tie them together by drawing on a narrow range of colors.

CLASSICAL BLINDS
▼ Ornate festoon or Austrian blinds need to be custom-made and take up a lot of fabric, but the final effect is perfect for these classical bow windows.

SWAGS AND TAILS

▶ The swags and tails on this window covering have been created by cleverly draping a length of fabric around a heavy wooden rod. However, do bear in mind the expense of such treatments — you will require a considerable amount of fabric.

Fabrics will also be used for occasional and dining table covers and napery, as well as for cushions and throws. Think practically, choosing fabrics that are easy to clean or launder if they are to be in a much-used situation. Such items often provide an opportunity to bring in some contrasting color accents to enliven a color scheme, or to provide a balance between patterned and plain surfaces. For example, cushions on a modern, square sofa upholstered in a plain fabric could include large, circular, geometric-patterned cushions, as well as conventional bolsters covered in a smart tartan check, and some square and triangular ones in plain, but interestingly textured, fabric. A Victorian *chaise longue* may be covered in striped mattress ticking and the cushion styles could include patchwork covers, embroidered petit point, silk with tassel trim, and velvet, all in a range of different sizes and shapes. A skirted circular table might have a layered look with a plain chintz cover to the floor in a rich color; a shorter floral patterned overskirt, and a lace or crocheted top layer. Don't underestimate the use of antique textiles for such accessories: these can often be picked up inexpensively at flea markets, yard sales and charity and specialist shops, and can be converted to elegant new use to furnish your living room.

For living room windows, options range from simple roller or Venetian blinds, to opulent swags and tails, trimmed with fringe and tied with tassels.The style of the treatment should relate to the architectural style of the room and the overall decorating theme. Conventionally, living and dining room curtains reach to the floor, but although this is undoubtably more elegant, it is not always practical. If there is a window seat or radiator under

COOLING SPACES
◄ A light, transparent fabric that allows sunlight to filter through is perfect for a south-facing room as the curtains can be drawn by day to create a cool atmosphere.

the window, for example, some compromise may have to be made. Cushions to match short, sill-length curtains might be the answer to the former; full-length curtains that are permanently on a fixed head held open with tiebacks, combined with a blind that pulls down to the top of the radiator might be the solution to the latter — or a second pair of short curtains.

The window itself also needs to be considered carefully. Small casements look better "dressed" with simple, short curtains, and tall, narrow windows might be made to look more interesting with a lambrequin fixed to the top of the frame, and blinds or sheers underneath to give essential privacy. Modern picture windows can take a streamlined treatment of neat, vertical Venetian, Roman, or other tailored blinds, whereas a Regency or Victorian-styled room will be enhanced by the traditional layered look of blinds or shutters close to the glass, a lace or sheer panel over this, and then formal drapes in a fabric such as brocade, silk or glazed chintz to finish it all off. If the room is small, and the windows are of different shapes, aim to unify them with the curtain treatment, using a similar style at all the windows, and choose a color and/or pattern that harmonizes with the wall behind. If the space, as well as the

VARYING THE TEXTURE

▼ Remember that the texture of your chosen upholstery fabric will affect the final color. Velvets, plain jacquard weaves or brocades will provide a denser color than a glazed chintz or cotton/linen blend.

windows, is large, then the fabric chosen for any blinds or curtains can contrast with the walls.

If the window is architecturally outstanding, and you would like to draw attention to it, choose a very simple treatment such as a screen or shutters that fold back into the window reveal to each side. If the window does not have to be covered for privacy or insulation, throw a sheer fabric such as muslin, voile or lace over a curtain rod, positioned well above the top of the window to soften the frame.

PILE THEM HIGH

▲ For luxurious seating, fill a sofa with a myriad of cushions. The throw arranged beneath this pile cleverly disguises a particularly old piece of upholstery.

Walls *and* floors

These are the largest areas to decorate or cover and so will be very dominant within the design scheme, despite the fact that they are broken up by other elements: walls are interrupted by windows, fireplaces and doors; floors by the furniture.

Before you begin, remember to relate the size of any pattern and depth of color to the scale of the surface on which they are to be used. Bold designs and strong colors work well on large floors and walls, and next to big windows; paler colors and less flamboyant patterns look better in smaller areas.

Aim to plan your scheme as professionally as possible. This means working from the floor up. The interior designer always tries to start with the flooring and works the scheme for the rest of the room around this, partly because a floor covering should last well through several different changes of decor.

Many people don't think beyond wall-to-wall carpeting, but this is not always a sensible option as a carpet in a dining area can become dirty fairly quickly, and areas in front of a sofa or favorite chair can be scuffed by television watchers. Instead, consider laying a hard, resilient or smooth flooring (wood, tiles, linoleum or vinyl) and use rugs to soften the seating areas.

If you do select a carpet, choose the very best you can afford. This means considering the fiber used in manufacture (wool and nylon are more durable than polyester); the method of making; the type of pile and number of tufts per square inch. A looped or close-cut velvet pile is more practical in areas of heavy wear; longer piles will flatten in use.

IN THE PINK
▲ A rough-textured natural flooring contrasts with the sleek blush of deep pink walls. Areas of wall that are broken up by a fireplace, as here, can afford such a strong color.

Also, make sure you choose a practical color. Mid-tones are better than pastels or very dark colors, as both show dirt and lint. And bold patterns can make a room look smaller, so a muted color and textured or mini-print design might be a better choice.

Natural floor coverings are also available (such as sisal, rush, and seagrass mattings, jute and coirs) with attractive, heavily textured surfaces, which are popular for living rooms. Although not as soft underfoot as carpet, they are extremely hard-wearing. However, they can be difficult to keep pristine as stains may become ingrained and dried food spills will need to be picked out with a knife!

The wall treatment in your living room will very much depend on the style of the room and whether you want to enhance the room's original architectural character or whether you prefer to superimpose a particular look on a rather bland room.

Floral patterned wall coverings in soft, faded colors will suggest a country cottage image. If the room has a chair rail, or if you can add one, a stronger, flowing floral hung above a painted dado area covered in paintable textured vinyl, gives a Victorian Arts and Crafts flavor; classical images in clear colors can create the Neo-classical look of a grand country house; simple painted paneling is typical of the Georgian era; clever decoupage treat-

BOLD FOCUS
▲ A boldly colored carpet provides the focus in this modern setting, while the striped cushions and piano stool cover echo the wood flooring.

IT'S A RIOT
▼ The subdued flooring contrasts with a riot of wall color provided by friezes and a pop-art painting. Note the second painting resting against the wall art gallery-style, as if waiting to be hung.

COOL COIR, RICH REDS

▶ The neutral color of the coir flooring and wicker table is enlivened by the magnificent rich reds of the tapestry which continues in the stripes of the wallpaper, the decorative coving and in the cushions and other accessories.

ments will echo the elegant style of an 18th-century print room; Oriental or Middle-Eastern patterns in rich, jewel-like colors can set an exotic theme.

There are many period flavors from which to choose, but your room — and your taste — may be modern in outlook. If this is the case, try one of the many Art Deco patterns on wall coverings, borders and stencils. The styles of the 1950s and 1960s are also making a comeback, and although walls were often simply painted, some strong geometric designs were also popular. These can be a printed wall covering, or may be painted like a mural. For a hi-tech or minimalist look, plain walls give the right ambience. Add texture or break up the color, as in color-washing, to create a further dimension to a plain surface.

Stripes, checks or other definite linear patterns can be used to help create an illusion of greater height or width. Bold, vertical stripes, for example, will make a low-ceilinged room look taller; whereas a strongly horizontal treatment (a frieze, picture rail, patterned paper or chair rail) will help adjust the proportions of a tall room, making it look smaller and more intimate.

There are also lots of different ways of decorating living room walls using paint. This could be a simple, but colorful, coat of latex paint; either flat or eggshell. Then consider personalizing the room with borders, stencils, panels, friezes or even murals. Or try sponging, ragging, or combing in paint; books abound on the subject. Practice on scraps of paper first, as some techniques are a lot easier than others to master. For a quick effect, sponging or colorwashing might be the answer; for those with more patience, try your hand at the more taxing paint effects like marbling or rag-rolling.

DURABLE WOOD

◀ Natural wood flooring can be an expensive option, but it is far more hard-wearing than any carpet and spillages can be cleaned easily. If you cannot afford solid wood, there are many excellent veneers on the market.

Storage *solutions*

BREAKING UP
▲ A wall of shelves that is given over entirely to books can have a dense, overpowering effect. Aim to break up the area by using parts of it to display much-loved objects.

When it comes to planning living room storage, you need to assess exactly which items you want to put away neatly — and which you might use as part of an attractive display on dressers, shelves, or inside glass-fronted cabinets. Take into consideration the size and weight of all the things you want to store. Large books, for example, cannot be housed in a flimsy, narrow-shelved bookcase.

Your lifestyle, the room's decor and its size and shape will all influence your choice of storage. In a room with projecting chimneys, for example, you can make maximum use of the two recesses for base units, or a desk with shelving above; or use them for display cabinets or an imposing bureau bookcase.

The wood or other finish that you select will also help you to enhance the style of the room. Pine or light oak shelving and other storage pieces will suit a country-style living room, but mahogany, cherry or walnut will add elegance to a more formal room. If your theme is modern, then a pale wood such as ash or birch, a contemporary paint finish, and modern laminates or industrial materials like rubber, steel, latex or chrome would all be stylish choices. And if none of these appeal, or are afford-able, you could combine secondhand pieces with built-in cabinets, all painted to blend with the scheme. You might even try a decorative paint finish such as ragging, marbling or stencil-ing to unify the various items.

Most living rooms need storage space for a wide range of items, from CDs and videotapes to children's toys. In a dual-

purpose room, you may need to house even more items, such as computers and stationery — or even spare bedding if the room is a studio or the sofa is to be used for overnight guests.

First of all, decide exactly what you want to put where, then measure everything. You could combine ready-made with custom furniture or dress up some junk shop finds. Whichever option you choose, remember to take your tape measure with you when you go shopping, or make a careful note when commissioning a carpenter. You will then ensure that the insides of any storage unit are as practical as possible.

DISGUISE
▲ Hide ugly hardware with elegant drapes hung from a decorative metal frame.

SLEEK SHELVES
▼ Glass shelving and modular wood cabinets provide ultra-modern display storage.

Focal *points*

ANTIQUE AND MODERN

▲ This beautiful fireplace is in itself a focal point. But the addition of a fine Victorian planter filled with foliage, and a striking modern candle-holder draw the eye in even more effectively.

SIMPLY DRAWN

▶ Sometimes a simple jug of flowers is enough to draw the eye to a particular feature — here, the old fireplace.

Most living rooms need a focal point around which the seating can be grouped effectively, since furniture is no longer ranged (as it was in the 18th century) around the walls and "brought up" into the room when required. Traditionally, in cold climates, the focal point was the fireplace or stove, but nowadays it may well be the television set. But there is no reason why an attractive view from a beautiful window, or a picture, mirror or mural cannot be an equally effective focal point. As with all good design planning, try to look as objectively as possible at the room to assess its shape, size and character. Aim to enhance its good features and camouflage the bad, and if an existing fireplace or window is worthy of attention, make it the focal point.

A fireplace is still seen as the warm, welcoming heart of the home, even if it is not used for a real fire. There are many alternatives, from gas-powered log-flame effects to wood-burning stoves. Look for a fireplace that is in keeping with the architectural style of the room; or if there are no obvious features, choose one that suggests a particular style. If you have an original fireplace, don't rush to pull it out. It may be possible to restore it, or if it is ugly, you may find a suitable replacement in a salvage yard. There are also many manufacturers offering reproduction mantels and fire surrounds.

In a room without an existing fireplace or chimney, a blank wall can often become a focal point. Fill it with storage units and shelves (see page 70-71), leaving a space in the center for a free-standing fire or stove, or in warmer climates, group plants, large ornaments or photographs in it, perhaps lit with dramatic display lighting. Other wall treatments can be used to create a similar effect, such as a tapestry, kilim or Oriental rug, hung from a curtain rod. Or create mock panels using beading or molding painted in a contrasting or complementary color to the main wall. You can perhaps fill the center of the panel with a different wallpaper or another harmonizing paint color.

If the focal point is the view from the window, then keep the dressing simple: shutters, blinds or a vertical screen. Remember that at night you might want something a little more decorative — alternatively, a view over a floodlit garden can be attractive.

SCREEN TO BE SEEN

▲ A stunning glass firescreen is the focal point of this room in summer. On cold days, the screen can be drawn aside, when the fire itself naturally attracts attention.

Lighting

BRIGHT COMBO

▼ In a living room it is essential that you don't limit yourself to one form of lighting alone. Strive to use both functional and atmospheric lights.

As most living rooms serve several different purposes, the lighting in them needs to be as flexible as possible. Aim to have several circuits, separately controlled, and to add dimmer switches to one or two of them, to help you adjust the lighting for different moods. Have plenty of socket outlets for table and standard lamps to avoid the problem (and danger) of trailing flexes. Other fixed lighting, such as wall lights and pendants, will need to be positioned to light various surfaces clearly. This is why a scale plan of the room (see pages 6-9) is so useful. It helps you plot the position of all the services accurately at the outset. As with most rooms, you will need to install the three

main types of lighting: general, ambient and background. If the room has a second door or access to a garden, dual-switch the lights to operate from both points of entry.

Task lighting is necessary to illuminate a dining table without causing glare, to light any desk area, to enable you to see to read or sew, and to see inside wall units and cabinets. Accent or display lighting can be used to light a picture, wall hanging or a floral display. It is also an attractive way of lighting a collection inside a glass-fronted cabinet, in an alcove or niche, or on display shelves. Light shining down or up through glass shelves is always effective. And don't underestimate the use of lighting above a window to enhance a beautiful fabric or interesting window treatment.

When you are selecting light fixtures or lampshades, always see them lit as well as unlit first. This is because the effect, especially on the color, can be totally different when the light shines through the fitting or shade. Most fixtures will be permanent, becoming part of the structure of the room. Others, like table lamps and standard lamps, are more easily portable, and are usually referred to as decorative lighting. Whatever lighting you choose, it should be in sympathy with the architectural style of the room and its decorations and furnishings. Spotlights in the ceiling, for example, may suit a hi-tech interior, but would look inappropriate in a period home or one with country cottage decor.

LOOKING FOR THE UNUSUAL
◀ Now that halogen light is being used more and more, the style of fittings is becoming increasingly wide ranging. Here, frosted-glass sails and a fine metal mesh add a soft and original filter to the white light.

CLASSIC LIGHT
▼ Chandeliers are the epitome of traditional elegance. Antique versions can be expensive, especially when rewired for today's use. For a less costly option, buy reproduction, straight from the shelves of lighting departments or home improvement stores.

Acknowledgments

The author and publishers would like to thank the following companies and their PR agencies for their kind assistance in the loan of photographs and props used in this book. We have taken care to ensure that we have acknowledged everyone and we apologize if, in error, we have omitted anyone.

For use of transparencies:
Domicil, page 11tr; Ducal page 11bl; Appeal Blinds page 54; Rolf Benz page 55t; Amdega Conservatories page 55b; Rolf Benz pages 62, 66; Pippa & Hale page 63t; Parador pages 71, 72 and 77t; 73b; Poliform page 73b; Pots and Pithoi page 59.

Picture Credits
Abode:7, 23t; 64; 74b
Phillip H Ennis Photography: contents/r; 8; 11tl (designer - Dennis Rolland Inc); 13b (designer - Barbara Ostrom Associates); 16 (designer - Audio/Video Interiors); 29t(designer - KAT Interiors/Kathleen Dickelman); 29b (designer - Vince Lattuca); 33 (designer - Barbara Ostrom Associates); 34 (designer - Marge Young Interiors); 36 (designer - Gail Green 11, Inc); 41 (designer - Bennett Weinstock); 69t (designer - Richard Schlesinger Interior Design); 73t (designer - SGH Designs/Stephen & Gail Huberman); 74t ; 75 (designer Vince Lattuca).
Rupert Horrox: 68
Interior Archive: front cover; Interior Archive/Mortimer 9; Interior Archive/Simon Upton 15, 22; Interior Archive/Schulenberg 21, 25t, 26, 38, 42, 45, 47; 67; Interior Archive/Pilkington 37t
International Interiors: Paul Ryan 19; 53; 61; 63b; 65
Mainstream: contents/l; 4/5; 12; 13t; 28
Elizabeth Whiting Associates: 1; 11br; 23b; 30; 37b; 49t; 49b; 50; 57; 69b; 70; 76; 77b;
Picture Perfect 48;
Zefa: 10, 58

Index